A LOVER'S
ALPHABET

First HarperCollins Edition 1993

LC 92-56112

ISBN 0-06-250832-6

93 94 95 96 97 XXX 10 9 8 7 6 5 4 3 2 1

WARNING: With the prevalence of AIDS and other sexually
transmitted diseases, if you do not practice safe sex you
are risking your life and your partner's life.

A LOVER'S ALPHABET

*A collection of aphrodisiac recipes, magic formulae,
lovemaking secrets and erotic miscellany from
East and West*

HarperSanFrancisco
A Division of HarperCollins*Publishers*

INTRODUCTION

This work is a pillow book in the original Japanese manner: a lighthearted anthology of sexual anecdotes and advice, with illustrations ranging from the delicately erotic to the frankly bawdy. It has few pretentions for itself; such points as it has to make are mainly old ones. The oldest point of all is that sex is worth writing about. In the West, the Greeks were writing about it from the second century BC. In the East, Indian love texts pre-date that by many centuries. The West has received most of its important ideas from the East; the Hindu is not only the oldest tradition of erotology in the world, it is unquestionably the richest. India teaches that men and women are complementary and equal. The wonders of Chinese eroticism and the magnificent Japanese tradition - lacking that fundamental assumption - cannot compare.

The West's traditional contribution to erotology - looked at nationally - closely parallels achievements in gastronomy. In other words Italy and France lead while the rest follow. This

holds good until the mid-twentieth century when the American scientist Alfred Kinsey began to publish his pioneering work. England's contribution to understanding our own sexuality - a sense of self parody and bawdy humour - is represented in this book by the drawings of Thomas Rowlandson. The theme which the artist returns to in drawing after drawing is the inherent absurdity of an unequal, male-dominated society: an important point which he makes well.

Apple

In folk magic a woman can enslave the man of her choice by sleeping with an apple next to her skin and then persuading him to eat it. Whether making the fruit into a dumpling, tart or turnover modifies the magical effect is not recorded

Astrology

Believers in this occult science can surprise and delight their lovers by kissing, caressing and even massaging those parts of the body associated with an individual's sun sign. If your lover is Scorpio, consult the appropriate chart in privacy

AUBERGINE

The classic dish made from this supposedly aphrodisiac vegetable is 'imam bayildi' which means 'swooning imam.' Whether the Turkish potentate fainted from gastronomic or sexual excess is not clear

AVOCADO

Aztecs called it 'ahuacatl' or testicle, an association which seems to have impressed the Spanish conquistadores who exported the fruit as a sexual stimulant

BATHING

An activity not properly understood by the British, who bathe regularly but seldom with others and even less frequently for pleasure

*B*AWDINESS
This is understood by the British who value it in their writers and comedians while rather neglecting the extraordinary drawings of Thomas Rowlandson (1756 - 1827)

Bird Finding Nest

The Chinese of the Ming period invented this sophisticated erotic game and gave it its evocative name. Its novelty comes not from the sexual drama itself so much as the enormous variety of open air stages on which it can be played

BOTTOMS

The buttocks were the primary visual sexual stimulus of our primate ancestors before the alternative attraction of breasts developed as our gait became increasingly upright. The Devil depicted by Felicien Rops (1833 - 1898) is clearly a traditionalist

CHAMPAGNE

Perhaps because it excites all the senses, champagne is the only wine for the bedroom. The rituals of champagne are similar to those of lovemaking. Tension is built up in order to be released: ineptitude can in both cases lead to premature ejaculation. Scent, taste, sound, the prickle on the tongue - all are intoxicating. In its more feminine forms champagne can even be made to blush

CHOCOLATE
Sacred to the fierce love goddess of the Aztecs, chocolate was regarded as a rare and powerful aphrodisiac in seventeenth-century Europe. The Sun King, Louis XIV, anticipated modern advertising by luring women to his bed with a gift of chocolates

CHARTREUSE
In its green form said to be an irresistible sexual excitant for women

CICADA FIXED TO A TREE
Rear-entry lovemaking in the Japanese manner - ferocious and elegant

DATES

Rich in vitamins, and having the same calorific value as sirloin steak, it is not surprising that this rather underrated fruit appears in many of the aphrodisiac recipes of the great Arab physicians

DILL

Romany herbal lore singles out dill as the most potent of all aphrodisiac plants

DISTILLATE OF LOVE

The old name for the clear, slippery substance secreted by glands surrounding the male urethra and released during the earlier stages of sexual excitement. A useful lubricant in foreplay games and an ingredient in many medieval love potions

Ears

Whispering in ears does not exhaust the erotic possibilities of these organs which can themselves join in the fun. Women in particular can be aroused by manipulation of their lobes, which is the forgotten purpose of heavy pendant earrings which provide constant stimulation

Eryngo

Also known as sea holly, the testicle-shaped roots of this plant were extraordinarily popular in Regency Britain as an aphrodisiac. Demand for candied eryngo was so great among the less sprightly bucks that one entrepreneur opened an eryngo factory in Colchester

EXERCISE

Although exercise fads driven by the marketing industry have reached epidemic proportions in the West, a simple sexual exercise practised in the East for millennia has been largely ignored. Repeated contraction and relaxation of the vaginal muscles may improve a woman's sexual technique by enabling her to grip her lover's penis. Some also maintain that it strengthens female orgasm and prevents prolapse

FEET

It is not necessary to be a foot fetishist to enjoy the erotic possibilities of feet. Our soles are ticklish because they are well-served with nerve endings: gentle foot massage to stimulate the hidden erotic triggers has long been practised by oriental courtesans

FISH

Aphrodisiac recipes containing seafood are common to all cultures and periods. A spicy fish stew is recommended by such diverse authorities as a Hindu sage and a Roman seducer: neither could have known that it would reach its apogee in bouillabaisse

FLORENTINE

As an occasional erotic treat a woman can hold the skin on the shaft of her lover's penis back from the glans as he moves in and out or her during lovemaking. The patisserie of the same name, while delicious, is less dramatic in its effects

Gamahuche

*The traditional French term for the intimate kissing
and tonguing of a woman. The technique - which some
prefer to call cunnilingus - is an essential skill in any
man's sexual repertoire, both as a preliminary and as
an end in itself. Tongues are better suited to the
delicacy of a woman's anatomy than fingers; if her
lover is sensitive enough to understand that, she should
resist the temptation to grab his ears or hair in
her enthusiasm*

GINGER

The hot, spicy ingredient in numerous oriental
aphrodisiac recipes. Always use the fresh root

GINSENG

One of the most widely available 'aphrodisiacs' with an impressive list of supposed benefits

HONEY

A glorious food which has also been used in its clear form to reduce over-lubrication in the woman and to add interest and purpose to a tongue bath (see entry)

HONEYSUCKLE

Maidens once slept with this powerfully scented flower under their pillows to stimulate prophetic dreams of the delights they could hope to enjoy when they were maidens no more

HOPS

Despite their macho connotations, taken in excess hops have a well-attested feminizing effect

HORSE

Much has been written about the extraordinary historical affinity between women and horses. The caricaturist Rowlandson explored it in his own way

INDIA

*The quest for sexual wisdom begins and ends in India.
In Hinduism, and in the even older oral tradition of
Tantra, sex is regarded as a sacrament: all lovemaking
echoes the divine union of Shiva and his eternal
consort, Parvati. The doctrine that male and female are
complementary, co-equal and co-eternal is perhaps
India's most important message for the West. At a
practical level, Hindu erotology anticipates many of the
findings of Havelock Ellis, Kinsey, Masters and
Johnson and later sexologists by at least two millenia*

JADE FLUTE

The delightful oriental term for what the occident calls 'fellatio' - a name more suggestive of a character in an Italian comedy or some obscure law of mathematics

JAPAN

'Shunga' - the erotic prints of Japan which appear throughout this book - are the fiercest erotic art any culture has ever produced. Exaggerated penises are wielded with the ferocious formalism of samurai swords. The Japanese erotic tradition has nothing to do with the 'equality' between men and women implicit in Hindu erotology: while it is exciting and dangerous, it has less to teach the West

KABBAZAH

Sheikh Nefzawi, shadowy author of The Perfumed Garden, *maintains that a man cannot experience ultimate sexual pleasure unless his lover is a 'kabbazah' which means 'holder'. Whether a woman not born with the gift to contract her vagina at will can learn to grip significantly is not certain, but any strengthening of those muscles is beneficial (see Exercise)*

KAREZZA

A general term for techniques delaying male orgasm. The universal mismatch between the fast male sexual response and the slower female response can of course be overcome with art and practice. Taken to extremes - as in some Tantric and Taoist practices - it may damage the prostate and there is evidence that sexual stimulation without ejaculation may be harmful

LANGUAGE

*When one culture conquers another, language -
together with traditional customs - tends to be forced
underground. Very often fragments of the original
language persist as taboo words possessing an even
stronger 'charge' for that reason. So it is with 'four
letter words' in English which are a relic of an Anglo-
Saxon inheritance. Indian love texts recommend the
use of 'strong and forbidden words' between lovers as
an aphrodisiac - an experiment not difficult to conduct*

LEAPING WHITE TIGER

*The classic Chinese rear-entry lovemaking position in a
culture which favours that approach. The involvement
of assistants and the venue are optional*

Mandarin Ducks

*A Chinese - and Japanese - sexual posture often called
'spoon fashion' in England and America from the way
the couple fit together lying on their sides. A leisurely
and undemanding posture, useful on occasions when
the man is fatigued*

Maraichignage

*The correct term for 'French kissing' which takes its
name from the Maraichins - inhabitants of the Pays de
Mont in the Vendée. Why the unsuspecting farmers
and fishermen of Brittany should have become
identified with the practice has not been revealed
by anthropology*

MIRRORS

No traditional bordello was considered fully furnished without mirrors. Even if contemporary interior designers have no wish to copy the red plush and 'empire' furniture, they should remember that mirrors can be recreational as well as practical

MUSIC

Many lovers use music to create a mood, but these delights are only for the virtuoso performer

NABOB

The harems of the great nabobs are an extreme example of serial sexuality as are the legendary exploits of Don Juan: both rather miss the point. The old saying 'A man who cannot find happiness with any woman is looking for another man,' and the anonymous painter (right) understood the psychology perfectly

ORALITY

The significance of oral lovemaking techniques lies not so much in the sensations and visual excitement they give the recipient - though this is of course important - but in the generosity of the giver. It is a gift of pleasure to another which also implies affection and intimacy. Some people can almost disown the actions of their sexual organs, becoming detached bystanders rather than participants: an attitude not possible with oral sex

Picnics

The contents of the hamper are less important than choosing a place where al fresco lovemaking is possible – the real point of lovers' picnics since the Romantic Movement first made them popular

PERFUME AND SCENT

The human brain reacts to smell even more quickly than it registers pain, and a considerable proportion of it is concerned with that forgotten sense. Consciously we may refuse to recognize the pheremones carrying sexual information from others, rejecting the messages as 'uncivilized' or 'animal,' but our unconscious mind receives the information nonetheless. Pheremones may play a greater part in love (or hate) at first sight that we can imagine.

Excessive use of deodorants unsexes us by disguising our body's natural sexual 'transmissions' of pheremones. But perfumes which react well with our natural scent can actually carry our individual sexual message further. Once you have found the right perfume for you, stay with it. Mixing perfumes is a mistake

PILLOW BOOKS

These are little books of sexual ideas and illustrations kept within the traditional Japanese lacquered wood pillow. For many centuries they were exchanged between lovers or given to young people as wedding presents: they are the inspiration for this book

POSITIONS

The age-old human concern with sexual 'positions' has a serious point. The Hindu author of the medieval Ananga-Ranga, written 'to prevent the separation of the married pair,' said that a husband 'by varying the enjoyment of his wife, may live with her as with thirty-two different women... rendering satiety impossible.' The Hindu view may be practical but not all their recommended positions are - many are only achievable by yoga adepts. The basic and more enjoyable permutations were described by many Roman writers and have been illustrated by enlightened publishers in the West since the beginning of printing

QUICKIE

Spontaneity is as important as variety in a sexual relationship...

RETRIBUTION

This may be the result as here, if spontaneity is not tempered with good sense - or blessed by luck!

SAVORY

The Romans cultivated this pungent herb - which they called satureia - only for its supposed aphrodisiac qualities. It was usually taken with honey, which could be mixed with wine. The culinary applications of savory are relatively recent

SWINGS

The sexual response in women is far more complicated and varied than in men. Many women feel pleasurable sensations (and can even reach orgasm) through the rhythmic changes in gravitational force experienced when swinging alone. Used differently - as in this Chinese garden - swings can also be used to satisfy the penis-centred male response

TOMATO

Once called 'Peruvian Apples' and grown as purely
ornamental plants, tomatoes, originally a native of
South America, are now cultivated throughout the
world. Together with many other exotic imports they
gained a reputation as an aphrodisiac. The herb basil -
also said to be an aphrodisiac - has a unique affinity
with tomatoes, which deserve their name 'love apples'
when sprinkled with the fresh herb

TONGUE BATH

An erotic game called 'The Tree' in Japan. Some lovers
prefer to lick honey or yoghurt from one another's
naked bodies; while doing so they might reflect that
'lechery' comes from the word for 'licking'

UTKALITA

In medieval India sexual amusements involving swings and pulleys were called 'Utkalita' or 'the Orissan.' The adventurous should be warned that the vulnerable hydraulics of male sexual hardware are less easy to repair than gymnasium equipment

VALERIAN

This perennial herb has long been used as an
aphrodisiac. Celtic women wore a sprig of valerian
between their breasts to attract lovers while witches
used 'cetwale' to entice young men into their beds.
Later it became known as 'drunken sailor' and was
used by tavern prostitutes.

Valerian is available as a herbal infusion but it
should only be acquired from a reputable herbalist and
the stated method and dose should be followed closely

VANILLA

One of Madame Pompadour's favourite aphrodisiacs,
together with celery and chocolate

VIOLIN

An instrument long considered a powerful weapon in the armoury of a seducer; the violin also has satanic associations and Paganini was accused of selling his soul to the Devil. This cartoon satirises both the violin and the wretched music teachers who were the butt of countless jokes in the eighteenth century

Warmth

Essential to satisfactory lovemaking because both comfort and nudity are . . .

Wine

A Roman saying held that 'Venus is lonely without Ceres (bread) and Bacchus (wine)'

BACCHUS ET ARIANE.

X POSTURE

This lovemaking position can be achieved by the woman sitting on her lover's lap facing him. Once penetration is achieved both partners lean back away from each other until they are lying flat on the bed

YARROW

A scented perennial herb used in love magic. If tickling your true love's nose with a yarrow stem causes a nose bleed then he or she will always be faithful - a painful experiment but one with a reasonable probability of success as yarrow stems can be quite stout

YIN-YANG

In Chinese philosophy these are the two opposite and complementary forces from which everything in the universe is composed: Yin is female, Yang is male. Yin is dark, negative, passive and receptive; it is symbolized by night and water. Yang is light, positive and aggressive; it is symbolized by fire.

In Taoism - Tao is the principle which unites the opposites - human sexuality is an interchange of the greatest significance. Sexual union, both symbolically and in the power which it generates, is the central drama of existence.

The Taoist view is that each individual is predominantly Yin or Yang and, irrespective of gender, is composed of both elements. Only by union with a complementary individual is equilibrium, and happiness, possible

ZULU STYLE

A form of lovemaking without penetration which young warriors and unmarried girls were once permitted in a traditional ceremony known as 'the wiping of the spears.' The young man could move his 'spear' to-and-fro between the girl's labia until they both achieved orgasm, but was not permitted to enter her. The success rate of this broadminded though precarious solution to the problems of adolescent sexual frustration may be judged by the fact that the greatest of all the Zulu kings, Chaka, was conceived during just such a ceremony